Author's

This book features 100 influential and inspiring quotes by Margaret Thatcher. Undoubtedly, this collection will give you a huge boost of inspiration.

1

"If you lead a country like Britain, a strong country, a country which has taken a lead in world affairs in good times and in bad, a country that is always reliable, then you have to have a touch of iron about you."

2

"Disciplining yourself to do what you know is right and important, although difficult, is the highroad to pride, self-esteem, and personal satisfaction."

3

"If you set out to be liked, you would be prepared to compromise on anything at any time, and you would achieve nothing."

4

"To cure the British disease with socialism was like trying to cure leukaemia with leeches."

5

"I've got a woman's ability to stick to a job and get on with it when everyone else walks off and leaves it."

6

"You and I come by road or rail, but economists travel on infrastructure."

7

"Any leader has to have a certain amount of steel in them, so I am not that put out being called the Iron Lady."

8

"To wear your heart on your sleeve isn't a very good plan; you should wear it inside, where it functions best."

9

"There is little hope for democracy if the hearts of men and women in democratic societies cannot be touched by a call to something greater than themselves."

10

"The facts of life are
conservative."

11

"It is not the creation of wealth that is wrong, but the love of money for its own sake."

12

"Freedom will destroy itself if it is not exercised within some sort of moral framework, some body of shared beliefs, some spiritual heritage transmitted through the Church, the family, and the school."

13

"Left-wing zealots have often been prepared to ride roughshod over due process and basic considerations of fairness when they think they can get away with it. For them the ends always seems to justify the means. That is precisely how their predecessors came to create the gulag."

14

"Of course, to be a mother and a housewife is a vocation of a very high kind. But I simply felt that it was not the whole of my vocation. I knew that I also wanted a career."

15

"It may be the cock that crows, but it is the hen that lays the eggs."

16

"Every family should have the right to spend their money, after tax, as they wish, and not as the government dictates. Let us extend choice, extend the will to choose and the chance to choose."

17

"There are still people in my party who believe in consensus politics. I regard them as Quislings, as traitors... I mean it."

18

"It's passionately interesting for me that the things that I learned in a small town, in a very modest home, are just the things that I believe have won the election."

19

"I'm back... and you knew I was coming. On my way here I passed a cinema with the sign 'The Mummy Returns'."

20

"You don't tell deliberate lies, but sometimes you have to be evasive."

21

"Look at a day when you are supremely satisfied at the end. It's not a day when you lounge around doing nothing; it's a day you've had everything to do and you've done it."

22

"I don't mind how much my Ministers talk, so long as they do what I say."

23

"It pays to know the enemy –
not least because at some time
you may have the opportunity
to turn him into a friend."

24

"Do you know that one of the great problems of our age is that we are governed by people who care more about feelings than they do about thoughts and ideas."

25

"To those waiting with bated breath for that favorite media catchphrase, the U-turn, I have only this to say, 'You turn if you want; the lady's not for turning."

26

"I always cheer up immensely if an attack is particularly wounding because I think, well, if they attack one personally, it means they have not a single political argument left."

27

"Christmas is a day of meaning and traditions, a special day spent in the warm circle of family and friends."

28

"Europe was created by history. America was created by philosophy."

29

"What Britain needs is an iron lady."

30

"Being prime minister is a lonely job... you cannot lead from the crowd."

31

"I love argument, I love debate. I don't expect anyone just to sit there and agree with me, that's not their job."

32

"No woman in my time will be prime minister or chancellor or foreign secretary – not the top jobs. Anyway, I wouldn't want to be prime minister; you have to give yourself 100 percent."

33

"If you just set out to be liked, you will be prepared to compromise on anything at anytime, and would achieve nothing."

34

"For every idealistic peacemaker willing to renounce his self-defence in favour of a weapons-free world, there is at least one warmaker anxious to exploit the other's good intentions."

35

"A world without nuclear weapons would be less stable and more dangerous for all of us."

36

"Watch your thoughts, for they will become actions. Watch your actions, for they'll become... habits. Watch your habits for they will forge your character. Watch your character, for it will make your destiny."

37

"Some Socialists seem to believe that people should be numbers in a State computer. We believe they should be individuals. We are all unequal. No one, thank heavens, is like anyone else, however much the Socialists may pretend otherwise."

38

"It used to be about trying to do something. Now it's about trying to be someone."

39

"They've got the usual Socialist disease — they've run out of other people's money."

40

"My policies are based not on some economics theory, but on things I and millions like me were brought up with: an honest day's work for an honest day's pay; live within your means; put by a nest egg for a rainy day; pay your bills on time; support the police."

41

"Platitudes? Yes, there are platitudes. Platitudes are there because they are true."

42

"I don't think there will be a woman prime minister in my lifetime."

43

"If you want to cut your own throat, don't come to me for a bandage."

44

"The battle for women's rights has been largely won."

45

"The problem with socialism is that you eventually run out of other peoples' money."

46

"What is success? I think it is a mixture of having a flair for the thing that you are doing; knowing that it is not enough, that you have got to have hard work and a certain sense of purpose."

47

"I too have a certain idea of America. Moreover, I would not feel entitled to say that of any other country, except my own. This is not just sentiment, though I always feel ten years younger – despite the jet-lag – when I set foot on American soil: there is something so positive, generous, and open about the people – and everything actually works."

48

"There is no such thing as society: there are individual men and women, and there are families."

49

"People think that at the top there isn't much room. They tend to think of it as an Everest. My message is that there is tons of room at the top."

50

"Constitutions have to be written on hearts, not just paper."

51

"I never hugged him, I bombed him."

52

"It is always important in matters of high politics to know what you do not know. Those who think that they know, but are mistaken, and act upon their mistakes, are the most dangerous people to have in charge."

53

"Any woman who understands the problems of running a home will be nearer to understanding the problems of running a country."

54

"There is living tapestry of men and women and people and the beauty of that tapestry and the quality of our lives will depend upon how much each of us is prepared to take responsibility for ourselves and each of us prepared to turn round and help by our own efforts those who are unfortunate."

55

"The choice facing the nation is between two totally different ways of life. And what a prize we have to fight for: no less than the chance to banish from our land the dark, divisive clouds of Marxist socialism and bring together men and women from all walks of life who share a belief in freedom."

56

"I just owe almost everything to my father and it's passionately interesting for me that the things that I learned in a small town, in a very modest home, are just the things that I believe have won the election."

57

"Whether it is in the United States or in mainland Europe, written constitutions have one great weakness. That is that they contain the potential to have judges take decisions which should properly be made by democratically elected politicians."

58

"Pennies do not come from heaven. They have to be earned here on earth."

59

"If... many influential people have failed to understand, or have just forgotten, what we were up against in the Cold War and how we overcame it, they are not going to be capable of securing, let alone enlarging, the gains that liberty has made."

60

"...The larger the slice taken by government, the smaller the cake available for everyone."

61

"Nothing is more obstinate than
a fashionable consensus."

62

"Whether manufactured by black, white, brown or yellow hands, a widget remains a widget – and it will be bought anywhere if the price and quality are right. The market is a more powerful and more reliable liberating force than government can ever be."

63

"I am in politics because of the conflict between good and evil, and I believe that in the end good will triumph."

64

"There can be no liberty unless
there is economic liberty.."

65

"To be free is better than to be unfree – always. Any politician who suggests the opposite should be treated as suspect."

66

"During my lifetime most of the problems the world has faced have come, in one fashion or other, from mainland Europe, and the solutions from outside it."

67

"We Conservatives hate
unemployment."

68

"There is much to be said for trying to improve some disadvantaged people's lot. There is nothing to be said for trying to create heaven on earth."

69

"It is one of the great weaknesses of reasonable men and women that they imagine that projects which fly in the face of commonsense are not serious or being seriously undertaken."

70

"To me, consensus seems to be the process of abandoning all beliefs, principles, values and policies. So it is something in which no one believes and to which no one objects."

71

"We were told our campaign wasn't sufficiently slick. We regard that as a compliment."

72

"...Conservatives have excellent credentials to speak about human rights. By our efforts, and with precious little help from self-styled liberals, we were largely responsible for securing liberty for a substantial share of the world's population and defending it for most of the rest."

73

"If my critics saw me walking over the Thames they would say it was because I couldn't swim."

74

"Oh, but you know, you do not achieve anything without trouble, ever."

75

"Defeat? I do not recognize the meaning of the word."

76

"To be successful you have to be selfish, or else you never achieve. And once you get to your highest level, then you have to be unselfish. Stay reachable. Stay in touch. Don't isolate."

77

"We want a society where people are free to make choices, to make mistakes, to be generous and compassionate. This is what we mean by a moral society; not a society where the state is responsible for everything, and no one is responsible for the state."

78

"I seem to smell the stench of appeasement in the air."

79

"The woman's mission is not to enhance the masculine spirit, but to express the feminine; hers is not to preserve a man-made world, but to create a human world by the infusion of the feminine element into all of its activities."

80

"Ought we not to ask the media to agree among themselves a voluntary code of conduct, under which they would not say or show anything which could assist the terrorists' morale or their cause while the hijack lasted."

81

"And what a prize we have to fight for: no less than the chance to banish from our land the dark divisive clouds of Marxist socialism."

82

"Democratic nations must try to find ways to starve the terrorist and the hijacker of the oxygen of publicity on which they depend."

83

"One only gets to the top rung of the ladder by steadily climbing up one at a time, and suddenly all sorts of powers, all sorts of abilities which you thought never belonged to you—suddenly become within your own possibility and you think, Well, I'll have a go, too."

84

"If it is once again one against forty-eight, then I am very sorry for the forty-eight."

85

"Most women defend themselves. It is the female of the species — it is the tigress and lioness in you — which tends to defend when attacked."

86

"One of the things being in politics has taught me is that men are not a reasoned or reasonable sex."

87

"I shan't be pulling the levers there but I shall be a very good back-seat driver."

88

"I love argument. I love debate. I don't expect anyone just to sit there and agree with me - that's not their job."

"Any woman who understands the problems of running a home will be nearer to understanding the problems of running a country."

"Being powerful is like being a lady. If you have to tell people you are, you aren't."

"Disciplining yourself to do what you know is right and important, although difficult, is the high road to pride, self-esteem, and personal satisfaction."

"I always cheer up immensely if an attack is particularly wounding because I think, well, if they attack one personally, it means they have not a single political argument left."

93

"What is success? I think it is a mixture of having a flair for the thing that you are doing; knowing that it is not enough, that you have got to have hard work and a certain sense of purpose."

94

"If you want something said, ask a man; if you want something done, ask a woman."

95

"I am extraordinarily patient, provided I get my own way in the end."

96

"To wear your heart on your sleeve isn't a very good plan; you should wear it inside, where it functions best."

"I usually make up my mind about a man in ten seconds, and I very rarely change it."

98

"You may have to fight a battle
more than once to win it."

99

"I've got a woman's ability to stick to a job and get on with it when everyone else walks off and leaves it."

100

"It pays to know the enemy – not least because at some time you may have the opportunity to turn him into a friend."

Made in the USA
Coppell, TX
05 December 2024

41850064R00056